JURASSIC WORLD

The Ultimate Quiz Book

Centum

UNIVERSAL
A COMCAST COMPANY

Jurassic World is a trademark and copyright of
Universal Studios and Amblin Entertainment, Inc.
Licensed by Universal Studios Licensing LLC.
All rights reserved.

Centum

2015 © Universal Studios Licensing LLC.

Published 2015. Centum Books Ltd.
Unit 1, Upside Station Building Solsbro Road,
Torquay, Devon, UK, TQ26FD

books@centumbooksltd.co.uk

All rights reserved. No part of this publication may be reproduced,
stored in a retrieval system, or transmitted in any form or by any
means, electronic, mechanical, photocopying, recording or otherwise,
without the prior written permission of the publisher.

CONTENTS

• JURASSIC WORLD ™

Twenty years ago, Dr John Hammond imagined a theme park where humans could finally come face to face with dinosaurs. He wanted everyone to be able to experience the wonder of the prehistoric world.

At last, his vision has become a reality. Thanks to him, you can gaze into the eyes of ancient creatures. You can reach out and touch animals that roamed the Earth millions of years ago.

After your visit, use this book to test every aspect of your new dinosaur knowledge and find out how much you've learned. You may surprise yourself!

General Knowledge Part 1

Let's start by quizzing your general understanding of the history behind our resort. Are you a dino dunce or a gene-splicing genius?

1 Imagine that the millions of years since the Earth began are just one hour on a clock. How long do you think humans have been on the planet?

2 Who first had the idea of building Jurassic World?

3 Which shark-eater lives in our lagoon?

4 What is a meat-eating creature called?

5 Which direct descendants of dinosaurs are still alive today?

6 What does a palaeontologist study?

7 What does 'dinosaur' mean?

8 Which baby dino can you ride in the petting zoo?

9 Which is bigger, T. rex or Spinosaurus?

10 What is a plant-eating creature called?

11 What does 'quadruped' mean?

12 At the end of which period did a catastrophic extinction event wipe out the dinosaurs?

Eras

To make it easier to date fossils, the years since the Earth began have been divided into five eras. Each of those eras is divided into periods. How much do you know about the different eras? Complete this table by putting the missing words in the correct places.

Then check the answers page to see if you're a budding geologist or an addled amateur!

MISSING WORDS

Carboniferous
Cretaceous
Devon
Fourth
Jurassic
New-born
Ordovician
Permia
Pre-Cambrian
Silurian
Wales

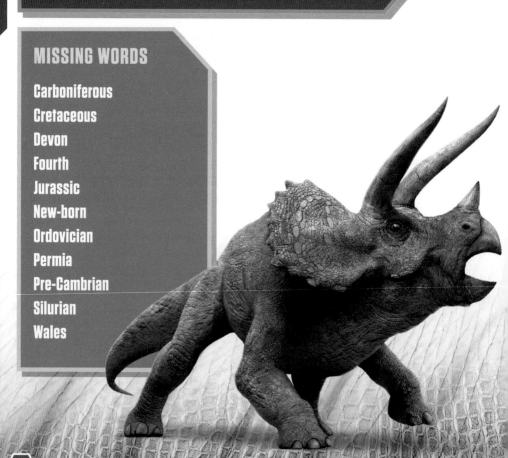

ERA	PERIOD	MEANING	LIFE
Archean		Before the Cambrian Period	Bacteria
Proterozoic			
Paleozoic	Cambrian	Named after Cambria, an ancient name for	Sea creatures and earliest fish
		Named after a Celtic tribe	
		Named after the Silures, a Celtic tribe	Fish
	Devonian	Named after	
		Coal-bearing	Amphibians and earliest reptiles
	Permian	Named after the ancient kingdom of	
Mesozoic	Triassic	Threefold	Reptiles, earliest birds, earliest mammals, dinosaurs
		Named after the Jura Mountains	
		Named after creta, the Latin word for chalk	
Cenozoic	Paleogene (*Paleocene, Eocene, Oligocene*)	Ancient-born	Mammals
	Neogene (*Miocene, Pliocene*)		Earliest humans
	Quaternary (*Pleistocene, Holocene*)		Humans

Fossils

So how do we know so much about the creatures that lived on Earth millions of years ago? It all started with fossils ...

1 **What makes a fossil?**

a. The remains of an animal, plant or organism, an impression or a footprint ☐
b. Anything over 100 years old ☐
c. A complete dinosaur skeleton ☐

2 **How did fossils get into rocks?**

a. The rock fell and crushed them ☐
b. The original animal was buried under mud or sand, which became solid rock ☐
c. The original animal knew a way to hide inside rocks ☐

3 **Where might you find a fossil?**

a. Floating in seawater ☐
b. In trees ☐
c. Underground ☐

4 **Which of these could be a fossil?**

a. A vast coral reef ☐
b. A pollen grain ☐
c. Both the above ☐

5 Sometimes a fossil dissolves away, leaving a hole the same shape inside the rock. What might get into the space to form a cast?

a. Minerals ☐
b. Concrete ☐
c. Water ☐

6 Which animals have been found buried deep in the snow and ice of the Arctic?

a. Penguins ☐
b. Mammoths ☐
c. Dodos ☐

7 Small prehistoric creatures were sometimes trapped inside what sticky substance?

a. Jam ☐
b. Resin ☐
c. Honey ☐

8 How may a fossil be removed from a rock?

a. By chipping around it with small hand tools ☐
b. By dropping the rock from a great height ☐
c. It can't be removed ☐

The Miracle of Jurassic World

It all began with a drop of blood. Follow our journey from the discovery of dino DNA to the creation of a completely new and monstrous creature.

If you've paid attention during your visit to the resort, you'll be able to fill in all 10 missing words.

Just one drop of _____ contains billions of strands of DNA.

A _____ strand is a blueprint for building a living creature.

Back in prehistoric times, mosquitoes fed on the blood of _____.
Some of those mosquitoes got stuck in tree sap.

When the _____ hardened, it could become fossilised and preserve the mosquito inside. This fossilised tree sap is called amber.

Jurassic World scientists took the animal blood from the mosquito and found _____ DNA.

A full DNA strand contains three _____ genetic codes, so it's a huge job to read it all. Luckily we have super computers and gene sequencers to show any gaps in the sequence.

If there are any _____ in the sequence, we complete the code with the complete DNA of a frog. This is known as gene splicing.

Sometimes, this _____ has led to surprising side effects. Some species have developed traits that they didn't originally have.

But our DNA adventures haven't stopped there. We know from using _____ DNA that we can splice the genes of different creatures. Now we have brought genetic material together from various dinos to create a brand-new DNA sequence and a monstrous new _____.

How Life Began

Dinosaurs are ancient creatures, but they are still much, much younger than our planet. Answer these questions and complete the story of the start of life on Earth.

1 **According to scientists, the Earth was formed about ...**

a. 4.5 thousand million years ago ☐
b. 5 million years ago ☐
c. 3.5 million years ago ☐

2 **For millions of years, the ground was ...**

a. ice cold ☐
b. molten hot ☐
c. underwater ☐

3 **The atmosphere was made of ...**

a. smoke ☐
b. steam and toxic gas ☐
c. oxygen ☐

4 Over millions of years, the planet cooled down and the ground became ...

a. grassy ☐
b. sandy ☐
c. solid ☐

5 The molten core of the Earth was closer to the surface than it is now, and the planet was full of ...

a. volcanoes ☐
b. rivers ☐
c. mosquitoes ☐

6 When the Earth cooled down enough for the steam to turn into water ...

a. everything was covered in ice ☐
b. it snowed until all the volcano fires were put out ☐
c. it rained without stopping for millions of years ☐

7 There was still no life on Earth, but slowly the atmosphere changed and the sun shone on the planet's surface. As a result of all the activity ...

a. the first humans appeared ☐
b. the land crumbled away ☐
c. the oceans had been created ☐

8 At last, the first living creatures appeared ...

a. on the land ☐
b. in the sea ☐
c. in the air ☐

Jurassic World Expert Part 1

Have you been paying attention? How much have you learned about Jurassic World during your visit? Answer these questions to discover how much of a park expert you really are.

1

What is the Gyrosphere?

2

What can you see at the Innovation Centre?

3 Is there a bamboo forest on the island?

4 What information is provided by the Innovation Centre?

5 What happens in the Creation Lab?

6 How are our flying creatures kept on the island?

Keep a note of your score and move on to the next part of the quiz.

7 What activities are available for visitors?

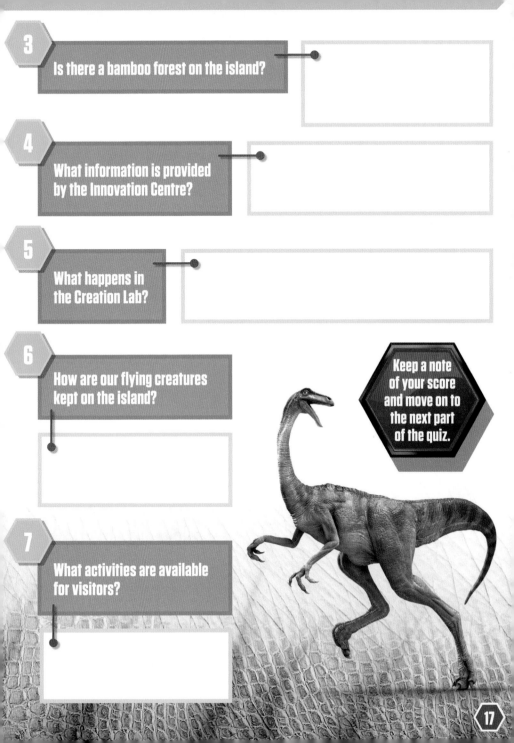

Sea Life

The first living creatures appeared in the sea, and they were tiny things like bacteria and viruses. What else can you remember about the first Earth-dwellers?

1 The small plants that started life in the sea released which life-supporting gas?

2 Which came first, fish or jellyfish?

3 The first fish did not have moving jaws so their mouths were always ...

4 Fish had a row of filters to strain what into their mouths?

5 Many fish had a shield of bony armour. Which part of the body did the armour surround?

6 Were most early fish small or large?

7 Of what were their skeletons made?

8 Slowly the fish with bony armour were replaced by fish that had [   ] all over their bodies.

9 Almost all modern groups of fish evolved from ray-finned fish, which had bony [   ] to support their fins. The other main groups were lung-fish and lobe-finned fish.

10 Which sea creatures have skeletons made of cartilage?

11 As the water level fell, what developed roots to be able to survive on land?

12 Plants died and were buried, where they slowly fossilised. What did they become? (Clue: we burn it to provide heat.)

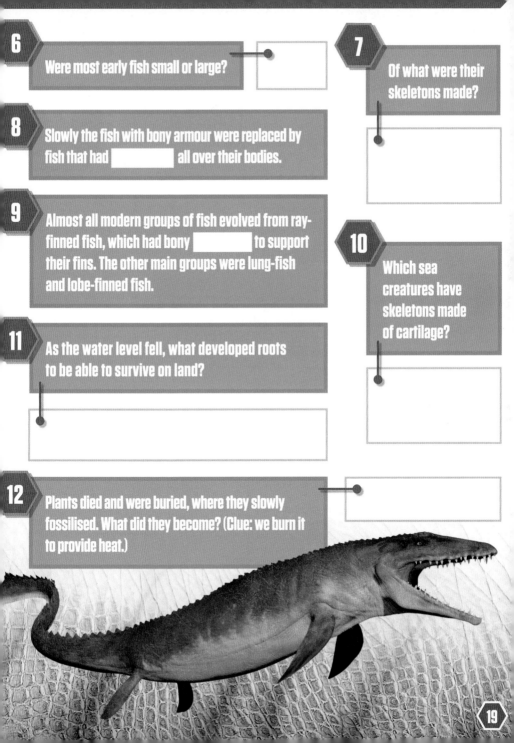

First Land Creatures

After millions of years, the first creatures left the water to make a new life on land.

1 What was the first group of creatures to leave the sea?

2 Scorpions, land snails and huge cockroaches lived among the plants on the land, as well as which eight-legged creatures?

3 Droughts began, and lakes and swamps began to dry up. So that they could breathe, some fish developed ...

4 The lobe-finned fish had two front fins and two back fins. What did they learn to do on these fins when their watery homes dried up?

5 What does 'amphibian' mean?

6 Did amphibians have fins on their tails?

7 As the swamps were lost and the planet became dryer, what new type of animal emerged?

8 Name the modern amphibian that was used by Jurassic Park scientists to fill in the gaps in dino DNA sequences.

9 At this time amphibians ruled the Earth because they were at the top of the ...

10 Some reptiles, like the Plesiosaurus, returned to the sea. What legendary monster may have been based on a Plesiosaurus?

11 Amphibians had to lay their eggs in water, but where did reptiles lay their eggs?

12 The fin-backed Dimetrodon is one of the best-known reptiles. Was it a herbivore or a carnivore?

Taking Flight

The reptiles that took to the skies are among the most exciting creatures at Jurassic World. How many facts can you remember from your visit to the aviary?

1

Various reptiles learned how to fly. Some grew feathers and their descendants are:

a. Birds ☐
b. Bats ☐
c. Penguins ☐

2

Some reptiles, called pterosaurs, glided through the air. Their wings were made of:

a. Tiny bones ☐
b. Feathers ☐
c. A thin layer of skin ☐

3

Name this crested flyer.

4

What was the main diet of the pterosaurs?

a. Insects ☐
b. Fish ☐
c. Berries ☐

5

Which of a pterosaur's fingers was longest?

a. Second ☐
b. Third ☐
c. Fourth ☐

6

What was special about the bones of the lightest pterosaurs?

a. They were hollow ☐
b. They were made of cartilage ☐
c. They were flat ☐

7

Where did pterosaurs live?

a. Caves ☐
b. Sea cliffs ☐
c. Nests in trees ☐

8

Name the flying reptile on this page.

Dinosaurs

At last the dinosaurs arrived, and for millions of years they ruled the planet. From plant-eating giants to small-but-vicious carnivores, they have fascinated humans since their fossils were first discovered.

1

Name this member of the sauropod group.

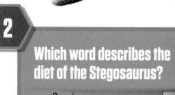

2

Which word describes the diet of the Stegosaurus?

a. Omnivore ☐
b. Carnivore ☐
c. Herbivore ☐

3

Which dino had a thumb spike?

a. Iguanodon ☐
b. Polacanthus ☐
c. Ankylosaurus ☐

4

The Stegosaurus was one of the first dinosaurs to:

a. Grow wings
b. Disappear
c. Walk on two legs

5

The swamps and lakes contained many crocodiles and alligators, which have changed very little in the millions of years since then. One difference was the position of their:

a. Eyes
b. Ears
c. Nostrils

6

On how many legs did Polacanthus stand?

a. Two
b. Three
c. Four

7

An early ancestor of Jurassic World favourite Triceratops had a bump on its snout but no horn. What was its name?

8

Duck-billed dinosaurs took the place of sauropods. They walked on two legs and it is thought that they were good:

a. Swimmers
b. Jumpers
c. Fighters

Extinction

The dinosaurs were the masters of the Earth for millions of years. No one knows for sure why they died out, but that hasn't stopped people from guessing!

1

The mass extinction marked the end of which period?

a. Jurassic ☐
b. Devonian ☐
c. Cretaceous ☐

2

The extinction is known as:

a. P–T ☐
b. T–K ☐
c. K–Pg ☐

3

Most scientists believe that the extinction was triggered by what event?

a. A massive comet or asteroid striking the Earth ☐
b. A huge volcanic eruption ☐
c. The movement of continents ☐

4

What percentage of species disappeared from the planet?

a. 25% ☐
b. 75% ☐
c. 50% ☐

5

Which continents were first affected by the event?

a. Europe and Asia ☐
b. North America and Africa ☐
c. All continents at the same time ☐

6

Some species were more affected than others. Which of these species survived best?

a. Alligators
b. Lizards
c. Pterosaurs

7

What percentage of bony fish survived the extinction event?

a. 75%
b. 90%
c. 30%

8

Where can geological evidence for the extinction event be found?

a. A thin layer of sediment in rocks around the world
b. A thin ring in tree trunks
c. Asteroids in outer space

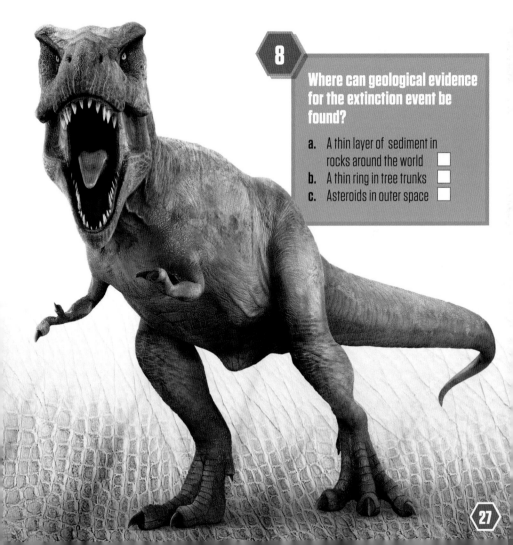

27

Jurassic World Expert Part 2

JURASSIC WORLD

Continue your expert quiz with these challenging questions.

1 Which animals can be found at the Petting Zoo?

2 What other creatures live in Gallimimus Valley?

3 What sort of vessel is used on the cruise?

4 How many visitors can Jurassic World take at a time?

5

Where is Isla Nublar located?

ISLA NUBLAR

6

What is the purpose of the botanical gardens?

7

How are dinosaurs kept off the golf course?

8

What happens in the Pachy Arena?

Keep a note of your score and move on to the next part of the quiz.

Prehistoric Mammals

After the dinosaurs became extinct, they left a big gap. What could possibly fill that space?

1

Two groups of animals emerged at the top of the food chain. Can you name them?

a. Amphibians and reptiles ☐
b. Mammals and amphibians ☐
c. Mammals and birds ☐

2

The earliest birds lived alongside the dinosaurs. Archaeopteryx looked similar to the birds of today in some ways, but one big difference was that it had:

a. Thumbs ☐
b. Teeth ☐
c. Scales ☐

3

Most of the first mammals were small and ate insects or seeds. Which of these was a little like a shrew?

a. Eohippus ☐
b. Phascolotherium ☐
c. Megatherium ☐

4

One of the most famous prehistoric mammals had enormous fangs, which it used to stab its victims in the neck. What was its name?

a. Sabre-toothed tiger ☐
b. Sabre-toothed cheetah ☐
c. Sabre-toothed lion ☐

5

The mammoth was an elephant with:

a. A hairy coat ☐
b. Small ears ☐
c. Webbed feet ☐

6

Millions of years passed, and the weather changed. The world began to freeze, and many mammals died out. This was the Ice Age, and animals had to be able to bear the cold to survive. Which of these was a woolly relative of the rhinoceros?

a. Ammonite ☐
b. Seymouria ☐
c. Coelodonta ☐

7

At last the planet began to warm up and the creatures that had adapted to the cold were no longer able to survive. Roughly how long ago do scientists think that the mammoths died out?

a. 50,000 years ☐
b. 10 million years ☐
c. 10,000 years ☐

8

Megatherium was an ancestor of the sloth. In which part of the world did it live?

a. South Africa ☐
b. South America ☐
c. South Asia ☐

Size Shuffle

Look carefully at this chart, and then fill in the names to see how much you know about the giants of Jurassic World.

15.2m long x 5.8m tall
a

13.4m long x 4.9m tall
b

2m

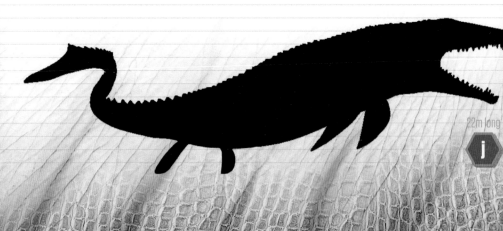

22m long
j

m long x 6.1m tall   2.1m wingspan

7.6m wingspan

c

h

i

9.1m long x 3.6m tall

d

3.6m long x 1.7m tall

f

9.6m long x 3.3m tall

g

e

4.6m long x 3m tall

a

b

c

d

e

f

g

h

i

j

General Knowledge Part 2

We want all our visitors to leave Jurassic World with a better understanding of dinosaurs and their habits. What fascinating facts have you picked up along the way?

1 When did the name 'dinosaur' first appear?

2 Did all dinosaurs lay eggs?

3 Were there dinosaurs in the South Pole?

4 Which American state is nicknamed the 'Stegosaurus State'?

5 Were the earliest dinos large or small?

6 What did Roy Chapman Andrews find in 1923?

7 Were there more plant-eating dinos or more meat-eaters?

8 Which Jurassic World dino has the smallest brain for its body size?

9 Which is bigger, Mosasaurus or a blue whale?

10 Why did some dinos swallow rocks?

11 Which Jurassic World dino has the thickest skull?

12 How many years ago did dinosaurs die out?

Dinos of the Future

We have brought to life some of the most incredible creatures that have ever lived, but there's still so much more for us to do. There are many species still to be reborn.

It's time to find out if you really know your dinosaurs. Read the descriptions and put each dino's name in the correct place. Perhaps you'll see one of them next time you visit the resort!

1 I have a big head and strong jaws, and I waddle when I run. I hunt in packs.

2 My name means 'false lizard' and I can live in water or on land.

3 I am a large sauropod with a long neck and tail, and four pillar-like legs.

4 I am a fishing bird with super-sharp teeth. I dive for my food but I can't fly.

5 My name means 'lizard of Alberta'.

6 I live in the water and my name means 'thin plate'. My neck is longer than my body.

7 I'm a fast, clever dino with sickle-shaped claws. My name means 'wounding tooth'.

8 I live in the sea and my enormous jaws crush my prey. My remains have mostly been found in Australia.

9 My name means 'egg thief' and I can run very fast. I am an omnivore.

10 I am a fierce ancestor of T. rex from the Jurassic Period.

11 I look like a dolphin, and my babies are born in the water.

12 My name means 'giant lizard of the south'. My teeth have saw-like edges and I am even bigger than T. rex.

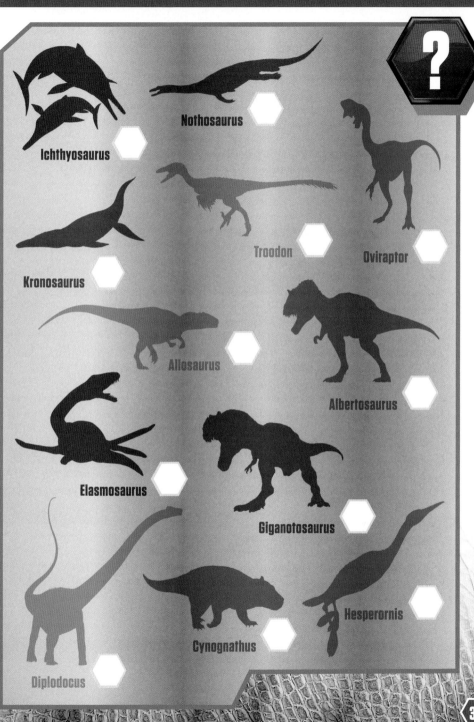

Ichthyosaurus

Nothosaurus

Kronosaurus

Troodon

Oviraptor

Allosaurus

Albertosaurus

Elasmosaurus

Giganotosaurus

Diplodocus

Cynognathus

Hesperornis

Jurassic World Expert Part 3

These questions will show how much you've listened to your Isla Guides.

JURASSIC WORLD

1 How much of the resort can be visited by monorail?

2 Which areas of the resort does the gondola lift carry you between?

3 Is it possible to ride a Gallimimus?

5 What creatures can be seen on the Cretaceous Cruise?

4 Which dinosaurs can you ride during your visit to Jurassic World?

6 What is the Egg Spinner?

7 How do we make sure that the T. rex cannot escape its kingdom?

8 Where does the Gyrosphere take you?

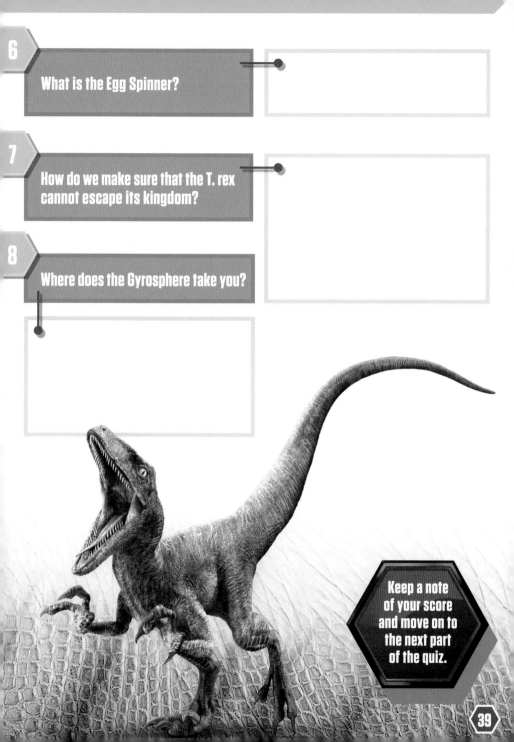

Keep a note of your score and move on to the next part of the quiz.

Species Quiz Ankylosaurus

1 What does the name 'Ankylosaurus' mean?

- **a.** Clubbed lizard ☐
- **b.** Fused lizard ☐
- **c.** Lizard hips ☐

2 What is its diet?

- **a.** Herbivore ☐
- **b.** Carnivore ☐
- **c.** Omnivore ☐

3 Where did it originally live?

- **a.** Europe ☐
- **b.** North America ☐
- **c.** Australia ☐

4 Dino intelligence is measured by the relative brain to body size. How would you describe Ankylosaurus's intelligence?

- **a.** High ☐
- **b.** Low ☐
- **c.** Medium ☐

5 It has four short legs that are larger at the rear than at the front. How many toes are on each foot?

- **a.** Three ☐
- **b.** One ☐
- **c.** Five ☐

6 What did this dino use as protection?

- **a.** Large teeth ☐
- **b.** Armoured body ☐
- **c.** Camouflage ☐

7 What is special about its tail?

- **a.** It's forked ☐
- **b.** It's clubbed ☐
- **c.** It doesn't have a tail ☐

Ankylosaurus

Species Quiz Apatosaurus

1 What does the name 'Apatosaurus' mean?

a. Deceptive giant ☐
b. Secret lizard ☐
c. Deceptive lizard ☐

2 What is its diet?

a. Carnivore ☐
b. Herbivore ☐
c. Omnivore ☐

3 Where did it originally live?

a. Africa ☐
b. North America ☐
c. Asia ☐

4 How big are Apatosaurus eggs?

a. Up to 30cm wide ☐
b. Up to 60cm wide ☐
c. Up to 90cm wide ☐

Apatosaurus

5 How does Apatosaurus move?

a. Running quickly ☐
b. Hopping ☐
c. Walking slowly ☐

6 How would you describe its teeth?

a. Like knives ☐
b. Like pencils ☐
c. Like bananas ☐

7 What does an Apatosaurus spend most of the day doing?

a. Sleeping ☐
b. Bathing ☐
c. Eating ☐

Species Quiz Brachiosaurus

1 What does the name 'Brachiosaurus' mean?

- **a.** Tail lizard ☐
- **b.** Leg lizard ☐
- **c.** Arm lizard ☐

2 What is its diet?

- **a.** Carnivore ☐
- **b.** Omnivore ☐
- **c.** Herbivore ☐

3 Where did it originally live?

- **a.** North America and Africa ☐
- **b.** Europe and Asia ☐
- **c.** Australia ☐

4 Which of its legs are longest?

- **a.** Front ☐
- **b.** Rear ☐
- **c.** They are all the same ☐

5 Where are its nostrils?

- **a.** On its neck ☐
- **b.** On top of its head ☐
- **c.** On its back ☐

6 What is Brachiosaurus's best defence?

- **a.** Its size ☐
- **b.** Its tail ☐
- **c.** Its teeth ☐

7 How many brains does it have?

- **a.** Two ☐
- **b.** One ☐
- **c.** Three ☐

Brachiosaurus

1 What does the name 'Ceratosaurus' mean?

a. Red lizard ☐
b. Horned lizard ☐
c. Spiked lizard ☐

2 What is its diet?

a. Herbivore ☐
b. Carnivore ☐
c. Omnivore ☐

3 Where did it originally live?

a. Antarctica ☐
b. North America and Africa ☐
c. South America ☐

4 How does Ceratosaurus walk?

a. On two legs ☐
b. On four legs ☐
c. It can walk on either two or four legs ☐

5 How many horns does it have?

a. Five ☐
b. Three ☐
c. One ☐

6 How intelligent is this dino?

a. Highly ☐
b. Average ☐
c. Not very ☐

7 How many fingers does it have on each hand?

a. Three ☐
b. Four ☐
c. Two ☐

Ceratosaurus

Species Quiz Compsognathus

1 What does the name 'Compsognathus' mean?

- a. Tiny jaw ☐
- b. Pretty jaw ☐
- c. Wide jaw ☐

2 What is its diet?

- a. Carnivore ☐
- b. Omnivore ☐
- c. Herbivore ☐

3 Where did it originally live?

- a. Asia ☐
- b. Europe ☐
- c. Africa ☐

4 How many Compsognathus fossils have been found?

- a. Fifteen ☐
- b. Four ☐
- c. Two ☐

5 How many toes does it have on each foot?

- a. Four ☐
- b. Three ☐
- c. One ☐

6 In which period did Compsognathus first live?

- a. Jurassic ☐
- b. Triassic ☐
- c. Cretaceous ☐

7 What sort of bones does it have?

- a. Bendy ☐
- b. Dense ☐
- c. Hollow ☐

Compsognathus

Species Quiz Corythosaurus

1 What does the name 'Corythosaurus' mean?

a. Amazing lizard ☐
b. Thin lizard ☐
c. Helmet lizard ☐

2 What is its diet?

a. Omnivore ☐
b. Carnivore ☐
c. Herbivore ☐

3 Where did it originally live?

a. North America ☐
b. Australia ☐
c. Asia ☐

4 Corythosaurus has a huge number of:

a. Teeth ☐
b. Claws ☐
c. Toes ☐

5 What does it use to produce its loud, honking cry?

a. Its arms ☐
b. Its nose ☐
c. Its crest ☐

6 Corythosaurus is a hadrosaur, so it has ...

a. Three stomachs ☐
b. A duckbill snout ☐
c. No teeth ☐

7 In what period did it first live?

a. Cretaceous ☐
b. Carboniferous ☐
c. Cambrian ☐

Corythosaurus

Species Quiz Dilophosaurus

1 What does the name 'Dilophosaurus' mean?

a. Bone-crested lizard ☐
b. Double-crested lizard ☐
c. Many-crested lizard ☐

2 What is its diet?

a. Omnivore ☐
b. Herbivore ☐
c. Carnivore ☐

3 Where did it originally live?

a. Madagascar and Australia ☐
b. India and Europe ☐
c. China and North America ☐

4 What does it have over each eye?

a. Nostrils ☐
b. Horns ☐
c. Two thin ridges ☐

5 How long is this dino when fully grown?

a. 6m ☐
b. 3m ☐
c. 9m ☐

6 Among the meat-eating dinosaurs of the Early Jurassic Period, Dilophosaurus was one of the:

a. Smallest ☐
b. Largest ☐
c. Slowest ☐

7 Which word best describes its arms?

a. Feeble ☐
b. Strong ☐
c. Gentle ☐

Dilophosaurus

Species Quiz Gallimimus

1 What does the name 'Gallimimus' mean?

   a. Chicken mimic ☐
   b. Turkey mimic ☐
   c. Ostrich mimic ☐

2 What is its diet?

   a. Carnivore ☐
   b. Herbivore ☐
   c. Omnivore ☐

3 Where did it originally live?

   a. Asia ☐
   b. Africa ☐
   c. America ☐

4 Is it bipedal or quadrupedal?

   a. Quadrupedal ☐
   b. Bipedal ☐
   c. Neither ☐

5 Its fingers are:

   a. Short and stubby ☐
   b. Short and thin ☐
   c. Long and slender ☐

6 What do we believe its top speed to be?

   a. 40mph ☐
   b. 60mph ☐
   c. 50mph ☐

7 Is it a predator or a scavenger?

   a. Predator ☐
   b. Neither ☐
   c. Scavenger ☐

Gallimimus

Species Quiz Indominus rex

1 **What does the name 'Indominus rex' mean?**

a. Unknowable ☐
b. Unbeatable ☐
c. Untameable ☐

2 **What is its diet?**

a. Herbivore ☐
b. Carnivore ☐
c. Omnivore ☐

3 **Where did it originally live?**

a. Isla Nublar ☐
b. Germany ☐
c. North America ☐

4 **Which dinosaur is bigger than Indominus rex?**

a. T. rex ☐
b. Apatosaurus ☐
c. None of the above ☐

Now you've seen the fearsome Indominus rex for yourself, write down your impressions here:

_____

_____

_____

_____

_____

_____

_____

Indominus rex

Species Quiz Mamenchisaurus

1 What does the name 'Mamenchisaurus' mean?

   a. Maiming lizard ☐
   b. Mother lizard ☐
   c. Mamenchi lizard ☐

2 What is its diet?

   a. Herbivore ☐
   b. Carnivore ☐
   c. Omnivore ☐

3 Where did it originally live?

   a. Peru ☐
   b. China ☐
   c. Italy ☐

4 How many neck vertebrae does it have?

   a. 11 ☐
   b. 16 ☐
   c. 19 ☐

Mamenchisaurus

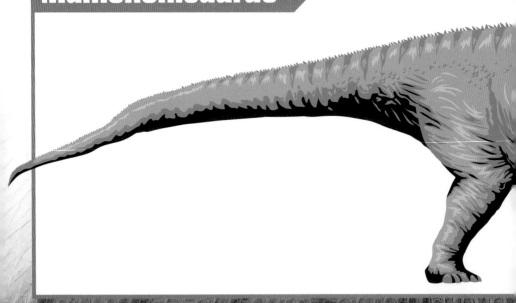

5 What shape are its teeth?

a. Spatula ☐
b. Dagger ☐
c. Pebble ☐

6 Of all creatures that have ever lived, Mamenchisaurus has the:

a. Longest neck ☐
b. Thickest legs ☐
c. Largest stomach ☐

7 In which period did it first roam the Earth?

a. Triassic ☐
b. Early Jurassic ☐
c. Late Jurassic ☐

Species Quiz Pachycephalosaurus

1 What does the name 'Pachycephalosaurus' mean?

a. Skinny lizard ☐
b. Foolish lizard ☐
c. Thick-headed lizard ☐

2 What is its diet?

a. Carnivore ☐
b. Herbivore ☐
c. Omnivore ☐

3 Where did it originally live?

a. North America ☐
b. South America ☐
c. Europe ☐

4 Who discovered Pachycephalosaurus?

a. William Parks ☐
b. William Winkley ☐
c. William Wright ☐

5 For what does it use its dome-shaped head?

a. Ramming attackers ☐
b. Digging for food ☐
c. Knocking down trees ☐

6 It has:

a. Large teeth ☐
b. Small teeth ☐
c. No teeth ☐

7 How thick is its skull?

a. 25cm ☐
b. 10cm ☐
c. 15cm ☐

Pachycephalosaurus

Species Quiz Parasaurolophus

1 What does the name 'Parasaurolophus' mean?

a. Near-crested lizard ☐
b. Small-crested lizard ☐
c. Feathered lizard ☐

2 What is its diet?

a. Herbivore ☐
b. Carnivore ☐
c. Omnivore ☐

3 Where did it originally live?

a. Iceland ☐
b. Japan ☐
c. North America ☐

4 Who discovered Parasaurolophus?

a. William Parks ☐
b. William Winkley ☐
c. William Wright ☐

5 It is what type of dinosaur?

a. Theropod ☐
b. Sauropod ☐
c. Hadrosaur ☐

6 How long is Parasaurolophus?

a. 2m ☐
b. 10m ☐
c. 12m ☐

7 How many years ago did Parasaurolophus first roam the Earth?

a. Over 70 million ☐
b. Over 50 million ☐
c. Over 7 million ☐

Parasaurolophus

Species Quiz Pteranodon

1 What does the name 'Pteranodon' mean?

a. Flying reptile ☐
b. Crested wing ☐
c. Toothless wing ☐

2 What did it eat?

a. Fish ☐
b. Plants ☐
c. Dinosaurs ☐

3 Where did it originally live?

a. North America ☐
b. Asia ☐
c. Africa ☐

4 What is a Pteranodon?

a. A dinosaur ☐
b. A pterosaur ☐
c. A hadrosaur ☐

5 Can it flap its wings?

a. No ☐
b. Yes ☐
c. Only three flaps per flight ☐

6 In which period did Pteranodon first live?

a. Late Cretaceous ☐
b. Cambrian ☐
c. Devonian ☐

7 When standing, its height is ...

a. 2m ☐
b. 3m ☐
c. 4m ☐

Pteranodon

Species Quiz Spinosaurus

1 What does the name 'Spinosaurus' mean?
- **a.** Protected lizard ☐
- **b.** Spine lizard ☐
- **c.** Spinning lizard ☐

2 What is its diet?
- **a.** Omnivore ☐
- **b.** Herbivore ☐
- **c.** Carnivore ☐

3 Where did it originally live?
- **a.** Europe ☐
- **b.** Africa ☐
- **c.** Asia ☐

4 This dinosaur is a:
- **a.** Sauropod ☐
- **b.** Theropod ☐
- **c.** Pterosaur ☐

5 Cold-blooded animals like this cannot regulate their:
- **a.** Body temperature ☐
- **b.** Breathing ☐
- **c.** Appetite ☐

6 Which best describes its skull?
- **a.** Small and narrow ☐
- **b.** Long and wide ☐
- **c.** Long and narrow ☐

7 What does it have on its back?
- **a.** Spikes ☐
- **b.** A sail ☐
- **c.** Fur ☐

Spinosaurus

Species Quiz Stegosaurus

1 What does the name 'Stegosaurus' mean?

a. Spike-tailed lizard ☐
b. Smelly lizard ☐
c. Roofed lizard ☐

2 What is its diet?

a. Herbivore ☐
b. Carnivore ☐
c. Omnivore ☐

3 Where did it originally live?

a. Europe and Asia ☐
b. Europe and North America ☐
c. Europe and Africa ☐

4 Which of these statements is true?

a. The Stegosaurus has long front teeth ☐
b. The Stegosaurus's bite is about half as strong as the bite of a Labrador ☐
c. The Stegosaurus has no sense of smell ☐

5 Because its front legs are shorter than its back legs, it is good at ...

a. Nibbling plants that grow close to the ground ☐
b. Catching small animals ☐
c. Digging ☐

6 An average Stegosaurus is about the size of:

a. A horse ☐
b. A dog ☐
c. An elephant ☐

7 How many bony plates are on its back?

a. 14 ☐
b. 10 ☐
c. 17 ☐

Stegosaurus

Species Quiz T. rex

1 What does the name 'Tyrannosaurus rex' mean?

a. Tyrant lizard ☐
b. King lizard ☐
c. Tyrant king ☐

2 What is its diet?

a. Omnivore ☐
b. Herbivore ☐
c. Carnivore ☐

3 Where did it originally live?

a. North America ☐
b. North Africa ☐
c. Northern Europe ☐

4 What is special about the T. rex's skull?

a. It has a brain cavity the size of a walnut ☐
b. It has holes to make it lighter ☐
c. It is two-thirds the length of its body ☐

5 Up to how many teeth may a T. rex have?

a. 70 ☐
b. 60 ☐
c. 50 ☐

6 What do lots of people believe about the Tyrannosaurus rex, which is completely untrue?

a. It is purple ☐
b. It lived during the Jurassic Period ☐
c. It has two hearts ☐

7 It has the largest neck muscles of:

a. Any dinosaur ☐
b. Any animal ☐
c. Any meat-eating dinosaur ☐

Species Quiz Triceratops

1 What does the name 'Triceratops' mean?

   a. Three-headed lizard ☐
   b. Three horns ☐
   c. Three-horned face ☐

2 What is its diet?

   a. Herbivore ☐
   b. Carnivore ☐
   c. Omnivore ☐

3 Where did it originally live?

   a. North America ☐
   b. Asia ☐
   c. Australia ☐

4 How many years ago did Triceratops roam free on this planet?

   a. 65 million ☐
   b. 70 million ☐
   c. 75 million ☐

5 How does Triceratops live?

   a. In herds ☐
   b. In a couple ☐
   c. Alone ☐

6 How much does Triceratops weigh?

   a. 4550kg ☐
   b. 5550kg ☐
   c. 6550kg ☐

7 What type of dinosaur is Triceratops?

   a. Ornithischian ☐
   b. Saurischian ☐
   c. Theropod ☐

Triceratops

Species Quiz Velociraptor

1 What does the name 'Velociraptor' mean?

a. Speed maker ☐
b. Swift seizer ☐
c. Fast killer ☐

2 What is its diet?

a. Carnivore ☐
b. Herbivore ☐
c. Omnivore ☐

3 Where did it originally live?

a. Central Asia ☐
b. East Africa ☐
c. North America ☐

4 Of what is a Velociraptor's tail made?

a. Soft, flexible skin ☐
b. Muscles ☐
c. Hard, fused bones ☐

5 When was the first Velociraptor fossil found?

a. 1913 ☐
b. 1933 ☐
c. 1923 ☐

6 It has three curved claws. Which is the longest?

a. First ☐
b. Second ☐
c. Third ☐

7 Do Velociraptors have wishbones or hollow bones?

a. Wishbones ☐
b. Hollow bones ☐
c. Both ☐

Velociraptor

How to Survive a T. rex Attack

Jurassic World is one of the safest places on the planet. We've worked hard to make sure that our visitors can watch dinosaurs in complete confidence. But if you were to meet a T. rex face to face, would you be able to survive?

1 Where should you be alert for a T. rex attack?

a. In the hotel ☐
b. On the golf course ☐
c. A clearing surrounded by undergrowth ☐

2 A single T. rex is on the loose. Is it harmful?

a. No, T. rexes only hunt in packs ☐
b. Perhaps. Stay near other visitors just in case ☐
c. Yes, T. rex is a solitary hunter. Run! ☐

3 Can you outrun a T. rex?

a. Yes, a T. rex only jogs when chasing prey ☐
b. Yes, a T. rex can run at 10 mph and I can run at 15 mph ☐
c. No, a T. rex can run as fast as 40mph ☐

4 What is the most dangerous part of a T. rex?

a. Its arms and claws ☐
b. Powerful back legs ☐
c. Powerful jaws and huge teeth ☐

?

5 You stumble across a half-eaten dino. Will a T. rex show up?

a. No, they only eat fresh prey ☐
b. Maybe, let's wait and see ☐
c. Yes, T. rexes like to scavenge as well as hunt ☐

6 A T. rex spots you on open land. What do you do?

a. Run ☐
b. Stand very still ☐
c. Look for something that will distract it ☐

7 Which is the T. rex's most powerful sense?

a. Hearing ☐
b. Sight ☐
c. Smell ☐

8 If a T. rex chases you to a lake, how can you escape?

a. Swim into the middle, T. rexes can't swim ☐
b. Swim across leisurely, T. rexes can't swim quickly ☐
c. Swim across but quickly! ☐

RESULTS

MOSTLY As
You need to pay more attention, or you're going to be dino dinner!

MOSTLY Bs
You have some good ideas, but when you panic you make foolish choices.

MOSTLY Cs
Impressive! You'd stand a fair chance of surviving until help arrived.

Dino Diet

Write the correct food group letter into the answer box next to each dinosaur numbered below.

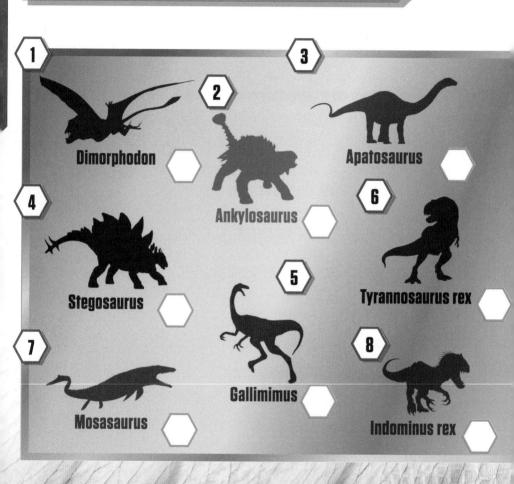

1 Dimorphodon

2 Ankylosaurus

3 Apatosaurus

4 Stegosaurus

5 Gallimimus

6 Tyrannosaurus rex

7 Mosasaurus

8 Indominus rex

GROUP A
EATS MEAT

GROUP B
EATS PLANTS

GROUP C
EATS FISH

GROUP D
EATS EVERYTHING

Velociraptor

10

Triceratops

Pteranodon

Dino Family Life

The dinosaurs of Jurassic World are not allowed to breed, but if they could, would you be able to recognise the offspring? After all, there's nothing as angry as a mother dinosaur protecting her babies!

Link each shadowy dino baby to its mother and bring the families back together.

Gallimimus

Velociraptor

Tyrannosaurus rex

Indominus rex

Triceratops

How to Survive a Raptor Attack

So you've survived a T. rex attack, but in some ways Raptors are even scarier. They hunt in packs and they're super-smart. Could you outwit the Velociraptors?

1 Where should you be most alert for a Raptor attack?

a. The botanical garden ☐
b. The lagoon ☐
c. Bamboo forest ☐

2 You're in the Jurassic World restaurant when Raptors burst in. Everyone panics. What do you do?

a. Look for the exits ☐
b. Join in with the panic ☐
c. Grab some cutlery and hide ☐

3 Three Raptors have cornered you in the hotel lobby. What's your plan?

a. Call for help as you run ☐
b. Surrender and hope they let you go ☐
c. Distract them by throwing something
   and then jump into the lift ☐

4 You run around a corner in the hotel and come face to face with a Raptor. What do you do?

a. Run back the way you came ☐
b. Scream! ☐
c. Dart into the nearest room
   and block the door ☐

?

5

A Raptor is one metre away from you in the undergrowth. What's your first thought?

a. Where's the nearest tree? ☐
b. Where's my camera? ☐
c. Where are the other two Raptors? ☐

6

You're two metres above the ground. Can a Raptor jump that high to reach you?

a. Maybe, I'll chance it ☐
b. No, Raptors can't jump ☐
c. Yes, move higher ☐

7

What is the most dangerous part of a Raptor?

a. Its sharp teeth ☐
b. Powerful back legs ☐
c. Large claws on its feet ☐

8

What is your best defence against a Raptor?

a. Run and call for help ☐
b. Stay still and it won't see me ☐
c. Throw something to distract it ☐

RESULTS

MOSTLY As
You have a small chance of escaping the Raptors, if luck is on your side.

MOSTLY Bs
Your chances of survival are nil. Perhaps you shouldn't have come ...

MOSTLY Cs
You know something about Raptors and that may help you to escape. Stay alert!

Identification

Can you identify all these creatures using only the picture clues?

1

2

3

4

5

6

7

8

Welcome to the final part of the expert quiz!
Complete these last questions and then
discover how much you know about the resort.

1 How long did it take to build Jurassic World?

2 What do we feed the T. rex?

3 How many sharks does the Mosasaurus eat every day?

4 Is the volcano in the north of the island dangerous?

5

What is the first thing you see when the ferry brings you to the island?

6

What gives you access to all our rides and attractions?

RESULTS

1–10

You haven't taken everything in, but that's OK! We hope you'll be back soon to learn more amazing facts. You are awarded a bronze Jurassic World Visitor's Badge. Congratulations!

11–20

Your knowledge of the island is impressive, and you have earned a silver Jurassic World Visitor's Badge. Congratulations!

21–28

You must have been to the island before! Your knowledge is amazing – you're as clued-up as our Isla Guides. Would you like to work on the island? You are one of the lucky few who can wear our most exclusive reward – the gold Jurassic World Visitor's Badge. Well done!

What Have You Learned?

After your amazing visit to our island of miracles, we hope that you will go home armed with lots more knowledge and understanding of dinosaurs. Now it's time to find out how much you've picked up along the way.

If you've been paying attention to the quizzes in this book, these final questions should be a breeze!

1 When creating dinosaurs, which amphibian's DNA is used to fill in any gaps?

2 When was the Earth formed, according to scientists?

3 What is coal made from?

4 The Loch Ness Monster may have been based on which reptile?

5 Did Proceratops have a horn on its snout?

6 What event happened at the end of the Cretaceous Period?

7 Which large prehistoric mammal was an ancestor of the sloth?

8 Which dino's name means 'wounding tooth'?

9 Does Ankylosaurus have high or low intelligence?

10 What does 'Brachiosaurus' mean?

11 On how many legs does Ceratosaurus walk?

12 How many neck vertebrae has Mamenchisaurus?

ANSWERS

Pages 8–9

ERA	PERIOD	MEANING	LIFE
Archean	PRE-CAMBRIAN	Before the Cambrian period	Bacteria
Proterozoic			
Paleozoic	Cambrian	Named after Cambria, an ancient name for WALES	Sea creatures and earliest fish
	ORDOVICIAN	Named after a Celtic tribe	
	SILURIAN	Named after the Silures, a Celtic tribe	Fish
	Devonian	Named after DEVON	
	CARBONIFEROUS	Coal-bearing	Amphibians and earliest reptiles
	Permian	Named after the ancient kingdom of PERMIA	
Mesozoic	Triassic	Threefold	Reptiles, earliest birds, earliest mammals, dinosaurs
	JURASSIC	Named after the Jura Mountains	
	CRETACEOUS	Named after creta, the Latin word for chalk	
Cenozoic	Paleogene (Paleocene, Eocene, Oligocene)	Ancient-born	Mammals
	Neogene (Miocene, Pliocene)	NEW-BORN	Earliest humans
	Quaternary (Pleistocene, Holocene)	FOURTH	Humans

Pages 10–11

1. a
2. b
3. c
4. c
5. a
6. b
7. b
8. a

Pages 12–13

Just one drop of **blood** contains billions of strands of DNA.

A **DNA** strand is a blueprint for building a living creature.

Back in prehistoric times, mosquitoes fed on the blood of **animals**. Some of those mosquitoes got stuck in tree sap.

When the **sap** hardened, it could become fossilised and preserve the mosquito inside. This fossilised tree sap is called amber.

Jurassic World scientists took the animal blood from the mosquito and found **dino** DNA.

A full DNA strand contains three **billion** genetic codes, so it's a huge job to read it all. Luckily we have super computers and gene sequencers to show any gaps in the sequence.

If there are any **gaps** in the sequence, we complete the code with the complete DNA of a frog. This is known as gene splicing.

Sometimes, this **splicing** has led to surprising side effects. Some species have developed traits that they didn't originally have.

But our DNA adventures haven't stopped there. We know from using **frog** DNA that we can splice the genes of different creatures. Now we have brought genetic material together from various dinos to create a brand-new DNA sequence and a monstrous new **dinosaur**.

Pages 6–7

1. One second
2. Dr John Hammond
3. Mosasaurus
4. Carnivore
5. Birds
6. Life before humans

7. Terrible lizard
8. Triceratops
9. Spinosaurus
10. Herbivore
11. Walks on four legs
12. Cretaceous

Pages 14–15

1. a
2. b
3. b
4. c
5. a
6. c
7. c
8. b

Pages 16–17

1. An orb-shaped vehicle that allows you to travel around the park
2. How science is shaping the past, present and future of our new Jurassic era
3. Yes
4. Everything you need to know about the Park
5. Dinosaurs are bred
6. Inside the Aviary
7. T. rex Kingdom, Mosasaurus Feeding Show, Cretaceous Cruise, Gyrosphere, Water Park, Spa, Golf Course – there's so much to do!

Pages 18–19

1. Oxygen
2. Jellyfish
3. Open
4. Food
5. The head
6. Small
7. Bone
8. Scales
9. Spines
10. Sharks and rays
11. Plants
12. Coal

Pages 20–21

1. Insects
2. Spiders
3. Lungs
4. Walk
5. An animal that can live on land or in water
6. No
7. Reptiles
8. Frog
9. Food chain
10. Loch Ness Monster
11. On land
12. Carnivore

Pages 22–23

1. a
2. c
3. Pteranodon
4. b
5. c
6. a
7. b
8. Dimorphodon

Pages 24–25

1. Apatosaurus
2. c
3. a
4. b
5. c
6. c
7. Proceratops
8. a

Pages 26–27

1. c
2. c
3. a
4. b
5. c
6. a
7. b
8. a

ANSWERS

Pages 28–29

1. Baby Triceratops, baby Gallimimus, baby Apatosaurus
2. None, only Gallimimus
3. A kayak
4. Approx. 20,000–25,000 visitors per day
5. Off the coast of Costa Rica
6. To preserve prehistoric plant life
7. Invisible barrier system used throughout the park
8. The dinosaurs put on a show breaking blocks with their head to show their strength

Pages 30–31

1. c
2. b
3. b
4. a
5. a
6. c
7. c
8. b

Pages 32–33

a. Indominus rex
b. T. rex
c. Apatosaurus
d. Triceratops
e. Gallimimus
f. Velociraptor
g. Ankylosaurus
h. Dimorphodon
i. Pteranodon
j. Mosasaurus

Pages 34–35

1. 1842
2. Yes
3. Yes
4. Colorado
5. Small
6. The first dino nest
7. Plant-eaters
8. Stegosaurus
9. Blue whale
10. To help grind up food in their stomach
11. Pachycephalosaurus
12. 65 million

Pages 36–37

1. Cynognathus
2. Nothosaurus
3. Diplodocus
4. Hesperornis
5. Albertosaurus
6. Elasmosaurus
7. Troodon
8. Kronosaurus
9. Oviraptor
10. Allosaurus
11. Ichthyosaurus
12. Giganotosaurus

Pages 38–39

1. All of it!
2. Between Bamboo Forest and Gyrosphere Valley
3. No
4. Baby Triceratops
5. Apatosaurus, Stegosaurus and Triceratops
6. A ride in the park, similar to tea cups
7. The T. rex paddock is made of 50' high cement walls and features an invisible barrier system for added security
8. Throughout Gyrosphere Valley to see the dinosaurs up close and personal

Pages 40–41

1. b
2. a
3. b
4. b
5. c
6. b
7. b

Pages 42–43

1. c
2. b
3. b
4. a
5. c
6. b
7. c

Pages 44–45

1. c
2. c
3. a
4. a
5. b
6. a
7. b

Pages 46–47

1. b
2. b
3. b
4. a

5. c
6. a
7. b

Pages 48–49

1. b
2. a
3. b
4. c
5. b
6. a
7. c

Pages 50–51

1. c
2. c
3. a
4. a
5. c
6. b
7. a

Pages 52–53

1. b
2. c
3. c
4. c
5. a
6. b
7. b

Pages 54–55

1. a
2. c
3. a
4. b
5. c
6. b
7. a

Pages 56–57

1. c
2. b
3. a
4. c

Pages 58–59

1. c
2. a
3. b
4. c
5. a
6. a
7. c

Pages 60–61

1. c
2. b
3. a
4. b
5. a
6. b
7. a

ANSWERS

Pages 62–63

1. a
2. a
3. c
4. a
5. c
6. c
7. a

Pages 64–65

1. c
2. a
3. a
4. b
5. b
6. a
7. a

Pages 66–67

1. b
2. c
3. b
4. b
5. a
6. c
7. b

Pages 68–69

1. c
2. a
3. b
4. b
5. a
6. c
7. c

Pages 70–71

1. a
2. c
3. a
4. b
5. b
6. b
7. c

Page 72–73

1. c
2. a
3. a
4. a
5. a
6. b
7. a

Pages 74–75

1. b
2. a
3. a
4. c
5. c
6. b
7. c

Pages 78–79

1. c
2. b
3. b
4. b
5. d
6. a
7. c
8. a
9. a
10. b
11. c

a) Carnivores
b) Herbivores
c) Piscivores
d) Omnivores

Pages 80–81

Pages 84–85

1. Tyrannosaurus rex
2. Stegosaurus
3. Dimorphodon
4. Triceratops
5. Velociraptor
6. Pteranodon
7. Mosasaurus
8. Apatosaurus

Pages 86–87

1. 3 years
2. Goat
3. Two
4. No
5. The Monorail Station that will take you to the entrance of Jurassic World
6. Bracelet scanner that serves as your entry ticket

Pages 88–89

1. Frog
2. 4.5 thousand million years ago
3. Fossilised plants
4. Plesiosaurus
5. No
6. Mass extinction
7. Megatherium
8. Troodon
9. Low
10. Arm lizard
11. Two
12. 19